The Journey to Find Me

A story of faith, transformation and finding my true calling

By Tonia Snowden

First electronic edition June 1st, 2017

Forward:

During this journey, I also wrote my memoirs alongside this story. When I was a teenager, I was told never to write a book about the things that happened in our house. The person who said that also said that if I did write it, they would come back to haunt me after they died. Imagine the irony when I learned, shortly after completing my memoirs, that the person who threatened me was now on their deathbed and given only six months to live.

Bio:

Tonia was raised by her Father and loving Grandmother until she was 12 years of age. Equipped with spiritual gifts she would learn to develop later in life, this is one of many personal stories Tonia will share with you.

Tonia's desire and calling is to show you what faith looks like through her eyes, and inspire you to recognize just how much power each one of us has.

With a notebook close by to record dreams, visions, answered prayers and faith.. she is guaranteed to take you on a journey that will inspire you to create and manifest your hopes and aspirations!

Tonia Snowden

TABLE OF CONTENTS:

And Miles to Go Before I Sleep

Before I started my journey from California to Memphis, I had a dream. In the dream, I was walking, just walking, down a road. It was during the day, and I was dressed for warm weather. I was only walking for a short time when it started to get dark. I looked up at the sky, and I could see the tops of the trees, which were extremely tall. That's all I could see...just the trees. It looked like I was in a forest.

When I focused ahead, I noticed that I was walking in the midst of all these trees, and the street I had been on was gone now. The curb I was walking on alongside it was gone, too. It was dark and cold. I was alone and afraid.

The path, once wide, was now closing in on me. A few moments later I realized that I didn't have any clothes on. That's when I saw a light alongside me. The light looked as if it were coming from a road alongside me. I started to walk even faster, almost running.

I could feel the Thorns from the trees and branches poking my body. Seconds later I saw just a glimmer of light. Suddenly, without any warning, all the trees were gone. I had reached the end, and it was daylight again. Little did I know that this was a warning about what would soon take place in my life as I started my journey.

Just Do It

So I'm sitting in my car thinking. Thinking about my current situation, thinking about the pros and cons, and not sure if I wanted to make a move, questioning if I was doing the right thing. I moved out of my apartment and had been approved for another apartment in a different state closer to my family.

I loved California, absolutely loved it. I loved the scenery, the freedom to be yourself, the supportive family that I had there. However, I needed a change. I'd been contemplating moving closer to my family for quite some time. Traveling back and forth every other month for a holiday, or birth of a grandchild made me question if it was time to move. A short time ago Southern California was a option because I was there attending a workshop a week just prior, and I loved it. The people in that area made me feel loved and supported. I felt as if I could make a go of it in San Diego. But always it was on my mind how much I wanted to be closer to my family, who were in Tennessee and Wisconsin.

Even though I found the perfect apartment in Oceanside just one block from the beach. But looking at what I would get for the money, it was exactly what I was already tired of. However, I knew that I could do better at my job, and I could make more money. But I wasn't certain that it was the best for me, because I would be starting fresh with no friends, no family, and I just wasn't feeling that way anymore.

I was looking forward to having some fun and enjoying my life, not a complete startup all alone again. That was not what I wanted. So this particular day I was sitting in my car and thinking that what I needed to do was to go and see the area of my new home, at least to see if I liked it or not. After all my new apartment was a manifestation of what I had drawn on my vision board months ago. I didn't have a home in California any more, so it wasn't like I had much of a choice. I kept asking and answering my own questions.

I said to myself, "I have a home. I have an address. And it's exactly what I put into the atmosphere, what I asked the Universe for, what I prayed for, and I received it. What is the hold up?"

I had a small amount of money, then, but I also had to go a long, long way. Finally, I said, "I don't have anything else to do." I told myself, "I'm going to drive 2,000 miles to my new home in Memphis."

I had a friend along the way that I could stop with if I needed to. However, I hadn't told my friend what I was doing. I needed to conquer this and make my own way. I needed to see and feel my strength. It was that feeling that I needed, to prove to myself that I could do it. I knew that I could drive it ten hours at a time, alone. Now I had to multiply that by three. It would take me three days to drive almost 2,100 miles, and I wasn't much of a night driver.

I went to the Dollar Store and grabbed some crackers, peanut butter, and cheese puffs. Then I went to the grocery store and got smoothies, water, bananas, and a supply of Red Bull. I had tried Red Bull a few times, and I knew it worked for me. I thought between Red Bull, prayer, and perseverance, I could do this. Right? I could do this.

It was three in the afternoon before I actually got on the road. I didn't tell my family I was coming, because I wasn't sure I'd actually make it. I was also keeping my options open. What if I made a stop and saw an opportunity? What if this just wasn't for me?

I got on the road, and I was praying. I just kept saying, "In order to receive change, I have to make a change. In order to take a step on my path, I have to make a change."

So once I got out of Southern California, there wasn't a need to call my friend. I didn't want to stop. I felt something inside me just kept pushing me forward.

I repeated aloud "Keep going. Keep going. I can do this. I'm OK. I'm not tired. I'm listening to good music. I feel good."

When it started getting dark, I felt like it was the true test, because I'm not a good night driver. There was an uneasy feeling coming over me. The music didn't sound as good. I felt doubt entering my mind.

"Am I doing the right thing? Should I turn around? This is stupid!" And then I said, "I'm working with what I have, and what I have is an address in another state. I have to go. What do I have to go back to California for? Nothing!"

I was using the GPS on my phone, but there was some construction in this area, and every time I would get off one highway, it would put me back going in circles. The GPS didn't know about the new construction.

I decided to exit, because of the construction. The road was closed and at one point there was nowhere to go. It was just me and an SUV left. We were just sitting there. Everything was blocked.

I started to get a little scared. It was not like being lost in the city. I was on the road alone, and my directions were not panning out. I would drive three miles, then take the next exit, only to go back in circles again. That went on for thirty minutes or so.

"I'll try to take another route," I thought. I drove to the very end, and there was no more freeway. It was nothing but a dirt road. It was just more construction. I turned around. When I looked at my GPS, it flashed another route, and when I saw that, I thought, "This is going to take me the long way, but I don't care. Right now I'm not getting anywhere."

I got back on the road and bypassed what my GPS was saying. Ironically, it led me exactly in the direction I needed to go in the first place.

Every time the GPS told me to get off here or there, I kept going, because I knew where here or there was taking me. I felt like the enemy was trying to discourage me. I was on the right path now. It was getting dark, but I felt better because I was on my way.

I needed to keep driving and driving. I didn't want to stop at a hotel. I just didn't want to do anything like that. I felt like a moving target. Stopping at a hotel late night in the middle of who knows where, being a single woman with only the front desk person knowing I was there didn't exactly make me feel like I'd get a restful night's sleep. My preference was to keep it moving and I get to my destination. That was the only way I was going to feel safe.

I was driving through states where I had no friends or family to come to my rescue. I needed to get through those states as fast as I possibly could. I drove until I couldn't drive anymore. I was tired, but I couldn't stop. I got a Red Bull at a gas station, and saw all these cars on the side. These people were all just in their cars sleeping. They were mostly families, and there they were in a 24-hour gas station.

I pulled in with everyone else. I felt safe there, actually. I leaned back in my seat to close my eyes and rest for a moment. I wasn't comfortable going to sleep, but I was comfortable being around these other people. I stayed there for around an hour or an hour and a half at the most. I just wanted to rest, but I didn't go to sleep. I actually went back inside the gas station and got some coffee. I thought I needed to keep going. "I can do this," I told myself.

I got back on the road, and talked to the Lord. I took my time. It was dark, very dark. Sometimes little or no light was visible going through small towns. I wanted to be extremely careful at the same time, trying to keep the scary thoughts out of my head. "What if I get a flat tire on one of these dark roads? Who's going to help me?"

Then I said, "Okay. There is no way the Lord is going to leave me out here, and allow anything to happen to me. The enemy is just trying to make me afraid, because if I am afraid, I might turn around and just go back. Then I would miss out on all the blessings that the Lord has for me at the end of this 2,000 mile journey." That kept me going.

Every time a negative thought came into my mind, I had to combat it with an A+ thought. A thought that I knew was an actual fact.

"I know the Lord will never leave me. He's never left me before, and there's no way he would leave me with no help on a dark road, knowing that I'm headed toward what he has for me. That makes absolutely no sense."

However, the human side, being a woman, driving alone, in an unknown state, where I knew no one, in the middle of the night, will take its toll on you as well, if you allow it to. Once I got through the first night of non-stop driving, I said to myself, "Lord, I can do this, right? Jesus, hold one hand. Lord, hold my other hand. And the Holy Spirit, hold my back to move me forward."

I may be in the flesh, but I know what the Lord is capable of. That's what stepping out on faith feels like for me.

Meanwhile, the weather was fine until I got to New Mexico. All of a sudden, the sky got the darkest gray, then black. And, of course, I was headed right into it. The sky looked almost like a tornado. Then to my right the darkness started to spread out in front of me, then on the side of me as I drove even closer. You could see that the darkness was on the sides and behind me. It was above me, too, as if there was a clear path for me to drive under what was happening above.

As I drove closer to it, I could hear hail, or a really hard rain. It started to hit the car. It just hit it and I couldn't even see to drive. It came down within seconds once. One moment it was clear, and within a couple of seconds I heard it, and a moment later it just poured onto my windshield, and I couldn't see. It caught me totally off guard. Again, my faith, my patience, my fear, everything was tested.

I didn't have tires for this. I was not equipped for this. My car all the sudden got freezing cold, compared to the warmth I had felt inside it just minutes before. I immediately looked for the next exit. I couldn't drive in this. I was sliding. I was on the freeway doing maybe twenty miles an hour, or less. The next exit, believe it or not, was probably a mile away

I got off at the exit, and saw the same type of gas station I stopped in hours before when I pulled over to rest. I prayed until I got to safety. I parked my car and took a breather for a few minutes. Within twenty minutes, I was able to get back on the road again, and everything was fine. All this time I still hadn't told anyone where I was. When my daughters would call, I would talk to them as if I were still in California, never telling them that I was on the road.

I never liked pop-up visits, myself. And here I was doing it to someone else. That actually played mind games with me, too. I didn't want to just pop up and say, "Hey. Here I am." Yet I needed to complete this journey, just me and the Lord. I needed to do that with only the Lord in the conversation.

Telling my family I was on the road alone, of course, created more confusion, so now I had their energy in my thoughts, and it shifted, or had the potential to shift, my destination, as well as how I got there, not to mention how I felt about getting there. I needed to see what I needed to see just for myself.

After I had been driving for twenty hours or so, my "Service Engine" light came on, then a little later, the oil light. I was more than 20 hours into the trip, so I thought, "I can make it. I've got like ten hours to go. I can do this. I can make it."

I checked the oil and it was low. I bought some new oil, and after having a problem getting the hood back down, I asked for help. The people that helped me were extremely nice. Both times I prayed and prayed. However, my prayers were not aloud. But they were thankful: thankful that I had the money to buy this $9 oil on the road. Thankful that the Lord put people there to help me. I got back on the road, and when my family called, I spoke with them.

The funny thing about when my family was calling was that sometimes I had to get off the road. Otherwise, they might have become suspicious. I needed my routine to be as it had always been.

So I was excited. I was getting pretty close to my destination, now. I was starting to feel a little more confident, because I knew that I was close enough that if something did happen, someone would come and get me, or I could take a Greyhound or Megabus. I can work this out.

Now I'm drinking these Red Bulls, right? So the second night, as I was driving, I kept saying, "I'm going to push it. I'm going to push it, and push it, and push it, and I'll make it to my destination by six AM, and I will surprise my family."

However, I was really tired, and I felt okay pulling over and just stopping and taking a break. But this time when I did it, I didn't feel comfortable. I moved to another parking spot, but I didn't feel comfortable there, either. There was just something about that place that didn't sit well with me. There were people around, but their energy was a little unsettling. I decided to drive a little farther, until I found another place where I felt more comfortable, and I talked to the Lord about it.

I couldn't feel good at this place. I knew it wasn't the place I should have been. Even leaning back in my seat didn't feel right. So I just kept looking around. I did go inside to get some food, though. It was the first meal I'd had in a day and a half. All I'd had since then was fruits, crackers, peanut butter, Red Bull, and water.

I went up to the counter and I saw all this delicious food. It looked so good, because I hadn't eaten any real food for over thirty hours. The guy behind the counter offered me more food than I had actually purchased. He said, "All these are good. Try this. I'll throw one in there. I'll throw this in, too." I thought, "Oh wow! That's really nice of you. I appreciate that. Thank-you."

Now you know that was nothing but the enemy. Let me tell you what happened. I went to the car, and I started eating. It was good. I only ate a very small amount, because I hadn't eaten for so long. I ate these potato wedges that were so big. I had never seen any that were this big before. Everything was just great.

I got back on the road, because now I needed to find a better spot too get a little sleep, or at least some kind of rest. I drove and drove and I felt myself getting tired again. It was dark outside. It was late at night, and I could feel myself drifting off a little bit now and then. I knew it was time to get off the road. I started praying: "Lord please put one of those gas stations in front of me that I was at once before. I felt very comfortable in that atmosphere."

I was tired and it seemed like it was taking forever. I would go past one exit, and it would just be a little small gas station. I went by another exit, and the gas station there would be closed. I said, "Lord, I'm tired. Please, please…"

It was fourth gas station when I saw it, and I was like, "Yes! Yes!" Praising the Lord quite loudly in my car. I was so exhausted, because I ate all that heavy food. That was a huge mistake on my behalf. I fell for the okey-doke.

I pulled off the road into the gas station, where I felt comfortable at last, thank the Lord. As I pulled in, I saw that the second spot from the entrance was vacant. I didn't even bother to go where everyone else was. I saw that spot and I pulled in. I let my seat back, and that's all I remember. I was so tired that I immediately fell asleep. I was just exhausted. By this time I had been driving more or less constantly for about thirty-six hours.

I woke up once, when I heard voices just outside. I looked up and saw people getting in, or maybe out, of the car next to me. I looked up, and I said, "I'm not going to be afraid, Lord. I know you, and you're protecting me." I just laid back in my seat and fell asleep.

When I woke up it was light outside. I believe it was around 6 AM, or so. I had slept for a couple of hours there in the parking lot.

I got more gas, went to the bathroom, got some coffee, and turned on my GPS. It said, "You are forty-six miles from the next exit of your destination."

I started to laugh, because I had driven all this way only to crash from what the enemy gave me to slow me down, and here I was, asleep at the goal line.

Back on the road it felt great, because I knew I had made it. I did it. I was only an hour away, if that. I was an hour away from my family. Everything made me laugh and smile. Everything that came on the radio, every song, every comedian, everything. It was a great and joyful morning.

I knew that soon I would be at my daughter's house. I knew that she had an appointment, and I was trying to make it there before she left. However, I didn't quite make it in time. When I got in front of the house, they were already gone. I called her, and she said that they were out.

I said, "I'm here."

She said, "Where?"

I said, "At your house."

She said, "Stop playing."

I said, "I'm not playing. I'm here. For real. I'm here in front of your house."

I kept going back and forth playing with her. Then I finally said, "I'm really here."

She started screaming over the phone, "You're here? No way!" I heard her tell her husband, "Turn around. We have to go back home. Mom says she's there, waiting for us."

I walked closer to the gate to play with the dog while I talked to her on the phone. She saw me under the security cameras and that's when she knew I was really there. That was the funniest experience that I cannot explain. It also was the real start of my journey. The drive was only the teeny tiny tip of what was to come.

My daughter, son-in-law, and the kids were taking care of business. I assured them I was fine waiting in my car. "Hey, I just drove 2,089 miles, so napping in my car in front of your home at 10 AM is just fine with me."

I took a blanket off my back seat to cover my face from the light and went to sleep. I was so excited that I had completed my journey. I had no expectations at that moment. I was in that actual moment of completion. I had accomplished exactly what I was supposed to.

And Now for the Memphis Blues

Two days later I went to the apartment complex where I was to sign my new lease and start my new life. When I was going down the road, I knew I was going to love it. It was on a road called Mud Island. Nice scenery of two rivers and some bike paths. It was perfect for me. Everything I had said I wanted: two bedrooms, two baths, washer and dryer, fireplace, top floor with a view, and huge square footage. However, something was missing. I wasn't sure what it was. Maybe, it was the fact that this was in fact my third attempt to move to Memphis, but the first time I made it. Or maybe it had something to do with the pipes bursting causing a flood in the apartment just several weeks go. Resulting in a delay, due to minor remodeling repairs. Whatever it was I couldn't quite put my finger on it. I went into the leasing office to let them know I was in town and that I needed a few days to work some things out before signing the lease.

The leasing agent was very understanding, and she said, "Okay." When I got in my car and drove away, there was a sigh of relief, partly because I knew I still had my address so I had a place to move into, and partly because I had time to actually explore the area a little more.

So one day my daughter and I were out taking a walk around her neighborhood. We came across this house that was for sale, and I wondered how much they wanted for it. It was pretty beaten up, but I was just curious, you know. What does a house cost down in this area? So as we were walking along, I started saying, "You know, I remember when I was looking at apartments, and I thought how affordable a house or how owning some property here would be beneficial. I knew that the market was very reasonable.

We kept walking and talking about other things. When we got back to my daughter's house, I sat on the couch and without even thinking I was led to pull out my phone and see. Hey, what is the housing market like down here? Now, you know I'm not thinking like the average person. I came here with very limited financial means. I did not have money for a down payment with me, or within my reach at that moment.

I did a search for condos and townhouses and for the options. That was the only thing I did. I wasn't looking for a single-family place. I was not really interested in the additional maintenance; never have been. So naturally, I wanted to see condos and townhouses. The very first property that popped up was a four-bedroom condo with three and a half baths and over 2,500 square feet. One ad said 2,500 square feet; another was listed as 2,900 square feet. I thought a four-bedroom condo? Isn't that a house?

I continued to look and read the ad, because it was on Craigslist and honestly, my first thought was this has got to be a scam. But there was a phone number with a name. If he's a scam artist, he's a good one.

Then I looked to see if it was on any other real estate sites for sale and it was, with the same name and number. So I called, and he answered. I was getting shocked left and right. When he answered, I said, "Hey, any chance you're showing the property today?"

It was a Sunday and I thought maybe he was having an open house. I was very honest when I said, "I just want to see what a four-bedroom condo looks like around here."

He agreed to show the property later that day. I was shocked again. Now it was starting to feel like fun. I was just going with the flow, keeping my options open, seeing what's out there with no expectations.

Really, I was just curious about a four-bedroom condo. There was a part of me that was thinking, "Why am I doing this? I want to see it, but why am I doing this? I don't have money to buy a house. I don't even have a job down here. Do you need a job and income to buy a house? Well, a lot of things had happened to me in my life that I couldn't explain, so those thoughts quickly dissolved.

First of all, the area was absolutely amazing. No matter which direction you went, there was something you want, need, or would like to eat. You name it, it's there. Entering the property it spoke of comfort and beauty. More of the same as I drove into the parking area and looked at the amenities. Then I saw that it was an end unit, away from everything. I can make as much noise as I want; I can do whatever

I want.

I was already excited. My family and I looked around and peek through the windows while we were waiting for the guy to show us the place. We all loved it before we even entered the property. My grandkids were saying, "Are you moving here?" And I was thinking, uhhhhhh. I responded that we were just taking a look at the property. We want to see what it looks like. Kids being kids, that wasn't good enough. Then they said, "Well if you like it, are you going to move here?"

I said, "We'll see." When we finally entered the property, it was nothing like I had expected. The basement area was an in-law suite. How cool is that? You can rent out this area. It's huge! In California the basement area, finished, with everything it has to offer, would go for over $2,000 a month, easily. I'm not in California, however. Having that option to offer that space to someone was great in and of itself.

After looking at it, I told the owner, "Hey this is really nice. I'm not in the market to buy a property, but I love this place. It's only $85 more a month than renting a two-bedroom, two-bath apartment on Mud Island."

Without even having to pray about it, I knew the Lord was giving me this property. Sometimes you just know. I told him that I needed a little time to get my things from California, and asked him if he would be willing to work with me. I explained to him how this was not my original intent.

He said, "Yes. Of course. I'm not in a rush to sell it. I'll work something out with you."

When I met this man, I felt as if we had met before. I felt like I knew him. He even looked familiar. That gave me a sense of comfort, that knowing Spirit recognizes Spirit.

He said he had to go away for a funeral, and when he got back we could go over the details. The following week he sent me a text message. We confirmed a time to get together. We went to the office and talked. I told him how much money I had when I was working, and what I was able to do. He worked it out with me, and we signed the deal. That's how I became a homeowner. Even writing this it still overwhelms me to think about that moment. I was blessed with more than I expected. I left California basically homeless. I didn't have a home in California and now I own a 2,500 square-foot condominium with the same money I came to town with.

Then came the icing on the cake: when I told him about my profession. He told me about another space that he had that was available, a business space. We left his office and went a few doors down. There I saw a space that was perfect for me, and I was given yet another huge opportunity to flow into something. There he was, giving it to me, again. It was overwhelming.

15

I had prayed for change, and then I made one change. Now look at this! It makes me want to cry. I had all my paperwork in the car as I drove to my daughter's to tell them the good news. I also had to thank them for letting me stay in their home for three weeks. I spent the first two weeks exploring, to see if this was a good area for me. I gave it two weeks, fourteen days. On the thirteenth day I walked into a condo that I now owned. The third week I spent looking at career business opportunities. I didn't feel stressed, because everything was flowing to me. The human side of me wanted to make sure that I did my part, and I did seek.

Movers and Shakers

Now it was time to begin the process of moving all of my things from California to Tennessee. I had a very, very tight budget of $1,500. I called to get a pod-trucking estimate. There was nothing under $2,500, and those all looked like scams. So I went back to an original thought.

Isn't it cool how it always happens that we have the answers with us all the time, but we're just not paying any attention to them? I called U-Pack, and was quoted a high price. I said that I couldn't afford that, and the guy said, okay, he'd give me a discount. And he cut the price *in half* to make it affordable for me!

Suddenly, the price was within my budget at $1,489. Now prior to this, I had prayed, and I asked God to get my things to me for $1,000. I couldn't do it, but I knew he could. When the guy at U-Pack said $1,489, I thought, okay. I'm not going to get any better than that, and I'm able to get everything I own to me for that price. I sent my keys from Tennessee to a friend in California, so that he would be able to open my storage space when necessary.

U-Pack arranged to drop off my unit at the storage facility two days later, which was a Friday. However, on Thursday they cancel, because there wasn't a unit available. Now normally, I would have been extremely upset because my plans changed, but I couldn't get that side of me out—that angry, emotional side. So instead, I just said, "Okay, fine."

U-Pack said they would reschedule everything for Monday. I let my friend know to be available Monday, and asked him to let the people in my storage unit know, too. I also called the storage company to let them know that my unit will be dropped off and picked up the following day. The woman wasn't the actual manager, but she said she would make accommodations.

Monday rolled around, and I got call after call that the driver is there with my unit at the storage facility, and they're unable to reach my friend who has the keys. They have been calling him for forty-five minutes, but getting no answer.

That wasn't like him. He is one of the most dependable people I know. I panicked, not knowing what to do, because I was 2,100 miles away. Then I called the manager at the storage facility, and asked her to show the driver where to place my unit. She called back a few minutes later and said she wouldn't allow him to leave the unit because it was too large and he had to leave. That put me in a panic again. My friend wasn't answering the phone, and my unit is unable to be dropped off at the storage facility. I'm liable to pay them, because I had to sign a contract. Now I'm thinking they're going to take my money and this is all I have down to the last dollar. This is it for me.

I got into my car and went to the bank to withdraw the money until I could figure out what to do. I withdrew the money, and went to the parking lot, and sat in my car. The best option for me at that moment was to have my things loaded on a truck and transfer them to the U-Pack terminal in Oakland.

Now that meant I would have to pay more money that I didn't have in my possession at the moment. Finally, my friend called as I was speaking to the agent, getting all the specific details. I told him what my options were, and he said, "Okay, here's what we're going to do. Call U-Pack back and tell them I'm going to bring your things to Oakland." We made arrangements to do just that.

Now, when would I receive my things? I was told six to eight business days. This was on a Monday, so another week or so without my things. Meanwhile, I was having to buy things that I actually owned already, but didn't have with me yet. I said to the U-Pack guy, "You guys cancelled on me Friday, the original day, so can you do something for me to get me back on schedule?"

He agreed to expedite my things to me free of charge. That's why it was meant for me to stay calm. My blessing was in that. Then he told me I get a discount for bringing my things to the terminal. The discount was $480. So the final invoice was for $1,009.

Now remember, I asked God to get my things to me for $1,000. Did he do it, or what? Look at this. My one change caused an effect I never imagined. Then my

friend told me he found someone to help move my things for $130. They made 3 trips to Oakland, which was 20 or 25 miles (depending on the location of the terminal).

Who does something like that? I was so grateful I couldn't find the words to express my gratitude. He even took pictures and showed me my things on the truck. Actually, he did that three times. He and I thought he would have to make five trips, but he met a guy who used to be a professional mover and he said he could pack it and make it in three trips and that's what happened. These were such emotional moments I hope that you can feel even a little bit what I was going through. Things were moved safely and with confirmed delivery.

There's No Place Like Home

The first day I got the keys and I went to my new home it was sweet. I stood there and looked at my fireplace, my kitchen, my ceiling fans, my home. *My home!* I have space for my entire family to gather together. Also, I had a brief moment when I thought, "Oh my God! What have I done?" I did all this without any money to spare. Should I have stayed in California?

Then there came a moment, as I was standing in the kitchen. It was a *déjà vu* moment. I had it again a few times in the house, and again a few days before I got the keys to the house. I was a mile or so down the street at a Starbucks. I wasn't parked directly in the Starbucks parking lot; I was off to the side in another area facing the Boulevard and other traffic.

I had been there before, so by the time I got to the house, and experienced the same thing, I knew I was on my way. I no longer doubted it. My spirit had already been here.

I did have that reminder to share my story. Actually, this is my second book. As I am completing this story, I also have memoirs that I completed a few weeks ago. This story I need to share. What I want you to know is that if I did it, you can do it. You need to know that. Please don't think it's a cliché.

When you go to work unhappy, or when you return home unhappy, when you look at your relationship with your family or your mate, when you look at your career decisions, when you look at your relationship with the Lord, or any other area, consider making one change—just one change. The Lord, or the universe, or whatever it is that you believe in, is pulling out all your blessings. They're just sitting in escrow. All your blessings are in escrow, and you're okay with that unless you decide to see how much you have in escrow.

I know it was meant for me to share this story, for at least one person. I'm babysitting my grandchildren, all four of them. I have more, but I have these four tonight. And they have been quiet, watching their movies, and then they quietly went to sleep without hearing anything from me. They knew I needed to do this for you. If you think the story isn't important, you need to read it again, without any distractions, with an open mind. Why? Because I'm no better than you, yet I have received so many unexpected blessings and they're still coming in, all because I made one change. I used to listen to people say things like that on TV and on different platforms, but it's nothing like that when you actually experience it for yourself. I'm sharing my private moments with you, hoping that you'll see you have a friend in me, one who supports and understands you.

Tonia Snowden

Memphis Blues Revisited

It was moving day. I got a call early in the morning, from a moving company offering to move me for twenty dollars an hour less than the company I talk to the day before. I made appointments with each company. When the cheaper company called me, of course, I took that one.

I was so excited. I can sleep in my bed tonight. I have my clothes, my sheets, all the simple things we take for granted. I longed for the scent of my own things.

I had Tupac's *Ain't Nothing but a Gangsta Party* blasting on my cell. It sounded real good to me. Yes I listen to all types of music. It keeps me in a good mood while sitting in California traffic every day. Plus music reminds of of happy times. I was smiling, as I got dressed, just knowing that I have options now. My clothes are here. Yayy!

I prayed over my home, because I didn't know these movers. Afterwards, I went to the U-Pack terminal. When I got out to go in the office to let them know to bring my unit, I noticed that the moving truck workers just watched me.

Then my cell rang. It was the movers asking if I'm the one in the Lexus. I said yes. Hello? My plates were from California, and I was the only other person out here besides the two of them. Naturally I think what's up. Hmmm. They followed me to the end of the terminal, and I got out to let them know my unit would be put in this space in a few minutes. That's when he disregarded what I had said.

He then said, "You know this is $65 an hour before we move anything?"

I said, "Look. I'm not about to play these games with you. He quoted me $45 an hour, and that's what I'm paying.

He said, "Oh. Well, I have to call and see."

I said, "Do that," and walked away.

When my unit came, the movers got out of the truck and proceeded to load my items. I walked up and just stood there. I believe the look on my face said more than it should have. He said okay about that price. After a few items were moved, the same guy brought out a clipboard.

"This is what I'm writing on your invoice: $45 for two hours. Anything after that is $65 an hour."

I said, "Why would you go up?"

He said, "He's already giving you a deal."

I said, "What does that have to do with anything? I'm the one who has to pay this, so I'm the one who needs to recognize if it's a deal. I know this game. I told you what he said. You wanna play this game?. Then two hours at $45 an hour and take all the heavy items out. Anything left, I'll put in my car."

He said okay. I got to my cell phone and called the office. I had to leave a message. I reminded the office about the quote they gave me. I also kept that text message on my cell phone. No one called me back, and the price didn't go up.

The crazy thing is, this guy did not give up. Even when we all got back to my home, and they were unloading, he started to tell me that some items I had to pay more for. To give you an example, I had my TVs in TV boxes, which are slightly smaller than my bakers rack boxes. The only reason he knew they were TVs is because I wrote TV on them, so that the movers would be careful.

I said, "I'm not paying for that. I can lift the TV box myself." I was close to telling him, "I can play the same game when it's time to pay, but I didn't.

The Lord has blessed me so much today, regardless of this.

He said, "Since we're not charging you to carry the TVs in, how about giving us a nice tip?"

Now the human side of me wanted to tell him how I really felt about him, taking advantage of a woman, but I didn't.

Actually, I felt kind of sorry for him, that this was the only way he knew how to make it in this world. I did give him a $20 tip, because I knew my Father has provided for me, will always provide for me.

Another thing that made it really good is that when I talked to U-Pack about this, they gave me an additional discount of $150. So that $150 was going to be credited back to my car. I actually spent that on the movers, so I was really doing quite well.

When you look at it that way, you have to be thankful and keep moving forward. The other interesting thing about moving is that both times my belongings were moved, I paid $130. In Oakland the guy charged $130. In Tennessee the moving company charge me $130, too.

Hmm...130? Again? After looking up biblical meaning. It read, new beginnings. Not good just new beginning.

After everything was done, I used my phone for all the things I needed to take care of. I was driving, and I noticed my phone wasn't charging in my car charger. I got home and I tried to charge it for a few minutes, and it just wouldn't work. It shut off, and I had to find a T-Mobile store.

Being new to the area, I had no idea where the nearest store was. I knew there were Sprint and Verizon stores, so there should've been a T-mobile store close by, too. I had seen those stores before in my area, so I drove to that area and asked a woman who was getting in a truck with her kids. She Googled T-mobile for me. How cool was that?

She got the address, but unfortunately neither of us knew where it was. I was still sitting at the stoplight when I heard a car horn. It was the woman telling me, "It's over here. Pull in front of me, and go that way. That's the direction of the T-mobile store." I thanked her, and thank God for a messenger.

I went to the T-mobile store and they quoted me a ridiculous price to fix my phone. I left, still without a working phone. I came home and sat down to have a cup of coffee. It was the very best moment. It felt so good to sit there in that chair, to feel the cushion, to see around me my most intimate things. Even my coffee tasted better.

I sat in the quiet with a ceiling fan going. I was in the moment, the phone the farthest thing from my mind. However, I knew how to handle my phone issue. I prayed.

I left the house and went to a Starbuck's so I could get online to send my family a message letting them know I'm okay and what had happened with my phone.

I emailed my daughter next, to get the name of the place she went to have her cell repaired when I was visiting the previous year. I was looking at other places, hoping to find something near my area, when my daughter email back with the name of the repair place.

She called and told them the part I needed. They said they had it and they also said how long it would take to repair it. They said to come on in. It was so funny. I had to write the directions down on a piece of paper.

I couldn't use the GPS on my phone, because it wasn't working. Now I do have GPS in my car, but that's another story why I never use it. I always use my cell phone instead. While I was waiting for my cell phone to be repaired, I read the manual so I know how to use the GPS in my car now.

My phone repair was slightly under $100. I also needed to get a new charger for my car and for home, because some of the fragments may have been in those charges and I didn't want this to happen again. Here we go again with the $130. The repair was close to $100 and the charger with $30. He actually gave me 5 bucks off. I was very thankful that I had the resources to get my phone repaired. Does it make sense to dwell on the fact that all of that happened? The guy who repaired it was super cool. He acknowledged that I was the one whose daughter called, and he did take very good care of me.

Then I Got the Message!

It was a long, but interesting day. Thoughts of frustration in my head. Why is it so difficult for me to receive a garbage can? Why do I have to leave my home to use cell? No cell signal even with signal boosters inside my home? Why no work for me since my arrival? It wasn't the first time I thought , Im not suppose to be here. While I was in the car waiting for my phone to be repaired, I thumbed through my notebook. On the sixth page, I saw just four words on the page and that was all. Those words were: passion, interest, expertise, and experiences.

I paused, then asked myself about those words.

Passion: I have a passion for healing the body. I also like telling stories.

Interest: I love to travel and to explore other cultures.

Expertise. I thought immediately about stepping out on faith.

Experiences: I wrote down "tell the stories." In that moment I felt a very new sensation and awareness. It wasn't like I was just sitting in my car. It was an indescribable awakening. I said, "Oh! I get it! I've been fighting to stay in my comfort zone working one on one, healing the body. because I love it so much. That's my passion helping others in making them feel better. However, my real purpose is to tell these phenomenal stories. True stories of dealing with hurt, pain and brokenness while still believing for something better. The stories people look forward to my telling them. I really didn't see how beneficial the stories were to others, until now.

Thank God for those quiet moments that teach us to listen. I seized that moment to make a commitment to record my stories on the day they actually happened, so that all of you could know everything.

Another small part of the story is that in the U-Pack office there was a woman next to me who asked me where I had moved from, and I told her.

She asked, "Why would you move here? There's a lot of crime here."

I said, "Crime is everywhere."

She said, "Where do you live?"

I told her Cordova.

She responded, "Well, they have crime out there, too."

Again, my face is saying way too much. She went on about how much it costs to live in California and how little you get , though she never lived there.

I said, "I know."

That's why I bought my property. I was a bit of a snot. I was proud to say that at the same time she needed to stop talking negatively about everything.

She said, "I guess that means you're supposed to be here."

I had to chuckle, because she gave me a confirmation. She was trying to discourage me, yet she was my confirmation. She was unaware what was actually taking place through her words. It was funny, because there were two guys in the office that we're working on my paperwork. And when I first went in, the guy said, "We don't know anything about your shipment." The woman said the same thing.

I said, "I confirmed last night, and again this morning. What do you mean you don't know?"

Yeah. I had a bit of an attitude. It was trying to rise, because I really did confirm, actually three times, to make sure that all my paperwork would be done.

The guys said, "We'll get it done...blah blah…" Then he folded his arms, as if to mock me. My arms may not have been folded, but I must admit that there was anger in my voice and eyes, because I thought, "How could you not know after I confirmed it three times! Not that many people work here."

I even knew the name of the person whom I spoke to the very first time, and she was there. But when he did that to me, it just reminded me that something was trying to get me riled up and ruin my day. That's when I let it all go.

I had been without my things all this time. The guy told me to go all the way to the end of the dock. After a few minutes nothing happened, so I walked all the way back to the office. By this time it was raining. The office crew was in total chill mode and said that he would be there and that I should go back. I did go back. Thank God for removing the thought to say, "I'm paying the movers and they aren't moving my things yet." I wasn't going to make a huge deal about any of it, and I didn't; yet everything was accomplished.

Looking for Answers

What's most important about this move is it cost me $130 on the California end, and when my things got to Memphis, the cost to move was again $130. I looked up the biblical numerology of 130 and in the book of Genesis it means life begins, new beginnings. Silly me. I thought that meant I was all good with the decisions I made.

During the entire time I lived in Memphis, I never unpacked, never set up my bed to sleep in. At the very beginning I slept on an air mattress, and later on my sofa in the livingroom. I watched movies on YouTube or played a DVD on my laptop. Even when my belongings arrived, both new 50-inch flat screens with theater sound stayed in boxes in the living room. I bought paper products so I didn't have to put my dishes in the cabinets.

Here I am in this 2,900 square foot condo that I wanted, and I wasn't comfortable enough in it to make it home. I lived on one floor. Maybe it was because in California you get accustomed to living in these tiny 500 square foot apartments. I felt like I was in someone else's home, and I would be leaving shortly. Even when my grandchildren slept over, the house felt the same.

You know sometimes you sleep better when someone else is in the house? Well, I felt the same discomfort, no peace, an unsettled feeling with or without company. Maybe I should've asked to sleep over at their house, instead.

Nothing worked out, not even simple tasks. No matter who I called, no one would deliver me a garbage can. I even called the Mayor's office. I did get a return call, but still no garbage can. I was told to call the same numbers I had been calling for weeks. My son in law had to come and load his new car with my garbage just to get rid of it.

I also had no cellular service. No calls over five minutes, and even then l had to call from outside the house and couldn't move or even breathe too hard. I used to sit in my car or drive toward the street to get a signal. I had an online profile where individuals could call and talk to me about family, goals, or relationships for a small fee. But I wasn't able to retrieve one of those calls. I didn't make one cent in Memphis.

There were times my mind wandered, and I would become afraid. What if something happened? I couldn't get emergency calls out on my cell. I had to keep pepper spray and a baseball bat within arms reach near the sofa where I slept. At one point I had a firearm to feel safe. But somehow, for some odd reason, it didn't feel necessary. My father in heaven didn't put me here to allow such a thing. It just didn't feel like it. I had to take back control of my mind.

No signal meant no way to have a little bit of income coming in. I had to find work since all of my usual resources were dry. Places I had normally worked before I moved to Memphis no longer needed my help. I did find a place that was hiring less than two miles from where I lived. The guy on the phone was great. I drove over there immediately after our conversation.

When I got there, an Asian woman was at the desk and when I told her whom I had spoken with, and I was here to apply for a job, she said they weren't hiring. I said I just spoke with him less than fifteen minutes ago. After a few minutes of calling her a liar, I was mentally exhausted and left. It didn't take long to see the handwriting on the wall. The message was loud and clear:

I'm not supposed to be here!

It's shameful to have to admit, this wasn't my first attempt to live here. The previous time, the pipes had froze and burst in the apartment I was supposed to rent. But this time was the furthest I had gotten. So, of course, I took that as a sign that it was time. Everything about my situation said, "Leave now. Forget red flags and tornado sirens going off."

Especially when I was sitting outside at a Starbucks one day. It was my favorite

Starbucks because the patio was large and covered, with dark brown wicker furniture and ceiling fans. It was like sitting in a sunroom at someone's home. It was inviting. There were always plenty of seats. I was looking online for jobs. I probably looked calm to the people around me, but on the inside I was in a desperate panic. I needed work, and I needed it badly. Right now! Today!

It was a nightmare. I'd never had a hard time getting work before. Not ever. All of my backup resources were gone. Now I was looking for a nine-to-five job, something I hadn't had to do for years. I didn't even know for sure what the protocol was for an interview anymore. I knew that if I did go on an interview, I would need to practice keeping my conversation short. Very short! So I'm looking, able, and willing.

That's when I got an email, then another, and another, all saying, "Thank you." I was puzzled. My face got all scrunched up. Why are these companies thanking me? Thanking me for opening my new accounts.

Then it dawned on me: ***OMG! My identity has been stolen!*** I jumped up from the table, threw all my things in my laptop bag, and ran to my car. I couldn't go home and make calls because I had no signal. I went into a panic. I called one place and they didn't even believe it was me.

That's when my daughter pretended to be me, without my knowledge. She knew I couldn't take much more. After speaking to a rep at one of the companies , pretending to be me she got more information than I did representing myself. How crazy is that? No such thing as security. She was able to get into my account, and saw my current bank info, driver's license, everything.

I went to the bank the next morning for many reasons. One, the crooks had a deposit scheduled to be made in an out-of-state account in a few days. They took out a loan. Hell, I didn't even know I could get a loan, but they did.

I kept saying, "I'm leaving." Driving in my car I would say it out loud, "I'm leaving."

The next evening I was just about numb when another bomb dropped on me. I was on my laptop, watching a movie, and I got hacked. An alarm sound came on, saying that my laptop had been infected with a virus. *All of my banking and personal information is exposed!*

A message was telling me to call Microsoft office at 800 blah blah blah. Now, I know the scam. But I didn't then, which by the way was less than six months ago. Yeah, I called, but of course the call dropped because I was at home and still had almost no cellular service.

When the fake Microsoft tech support number showed up on my cell as a scam or fraud, that confirmed my suspicion of the conversation I had with the tech just minutes before. Not being a technical person, I've asked for help a lot in the past, and this guy didn't sound like any of the techs I was used to. Again came the message. "I know. I'm leaving."

Nothing was working for me. The life I desired was not in here in Memphis. Did I leave it all in California? I haven't had any fun since I left. Not even a date. Not that I could afford the gas to drive to see anyone. Surely doesn't feel like my fate lies here.

Well, with the money I had in my pocket, either it would magically multiply or I had to do something quick. With bills due and my appetite. I ended up flying to California for several days to work. To some, that's extreme, but I invested in myself. Otherwise I would've drowned.

I arrived in Oakland at ten AM, and worked non-stop for twenty-four hours. It was well worth the $300 I had spent to fly back. Then it was around the fourth day when the money and positive energy flowing through and around me made me ask, "Did I leave my future mate here too?"

Yes, I went to an online dating site. I spoke with two great guys. One met me later that day. The other one I just blew off. However they both were part of my entire journey. That's all I'll say about them for now, but it's an amazing story that caught me off guard.

It is time to go! I'm leaving Memphis. I've done all I can do with no income and no phone service for starters.

Moving Day...Again

Moving day was also my granddaughter's birthday. Everything was set—movers would be there and gone within an hour or so to spare before the birthday celebration began. The movers were due at eight AM. I sold my big pieces of furniture; so loading shouldn't take more than an hour at most. The storage facility I was using was less than two miles from the house. You go down one street and that's it. The only turn was at the light, and then into the parking lot. Simple enough. Then I could join the birthday lunch and outing. I was definitely looking forward to having some fun. I hadn't laughed much lately. I used to be called silly and sometimes goofy. Now, I could hardly remember the last time I had a good laugh.

I got a call early that morning, not that I was in a deep sleep. I hadn't been sleeping well for a while. When I don't fall asleep until four AM, and am awakened at six AM, I'm sleepy. It was the moving guy calling to confirm a time. We agreed, and he hung up.

Interesting about this moving company. I was at a stoplight a few weeks earlier, and next to me was a nice white clean truck with a cool slogan written across the door. For no particular reason, I smiled at the truck. So when I looked on Craigslist for a moving company, that's the company that I called. But I didn't know it was the same company right away, because it was under the previous owner's name on Craigslist. What a coincidence, if you believe in that sort of thing.

It was after 8:00, and no moving truck in sight. By 8:30 I was pacing back and forth, looking out the window and trying to reconfigure the timeline for the day. I even started to slide boxes across the living room floor into the kitchen in front of the patio door. I just assumed it would be easier to load from the patio that led to the garage and driveway area. Having had less than four hours of sleep, no appetite (besides the hunger to move), I was getting a little panicky.

I stepped outside to call the moving company, and was told that they had no idea where the driver was, but that he was their best guy. Really? This is your *best*?

I explained that I had other appointments in addition to a woman who was to meet me at the storage facility to buy my oversized sofas. When I spoke with the owner of the company, he explained that he was out of town. Which actually meant that he was two hours away in the next city.

Dude you're in the same state. It's your company. He told me to consider finding another mover since he was unable to reach the driver. He also had the audacity to say that if the driver showed up, I have to pay extra to take the sofas to storage. That's when I let him have it. I called him unprofessional with no business etiquette. It's his company's fault. My plans have to be altered. He said, "Okay. What do you feel is fair?"

I said, "Send someone to get my things!" Ten minutes later I got a call. The guy on the other end was apologizing to me, saying he fell back to sleep, but he assured me I won't miss my other appointments. It was a few minutes after ten when he arrived.

The woman who was buying my sofas sent me a text saying she and a helper were on their way to the storage facility. Not knowing these people, I felt safer meeting them at the storage place instead of at my home, even though I was about to leave town.

I could barely sleep as it was, but with strangers knowing that I'm in a huge house all alone, in a state I had just made my home, just made it that much worse. I preferred to meet at the storage facility. I told the mover I had to be at my granddaughter's birthday celebration at noon. He said he could do that.

I helped, and we went as fast as our arms would move. I pushed boxes and boxes out the patio door as he stacked them into the truck. Even with our best efforts, I had no choice but to allow the strangers to come to my home to purchase the sofas. The idea of it made me queasy. At least the mover guy was here. I sent a text to the woman telling her that I was less than two miles away and to come to the house.

Several minutes later, a huge, new looking, shiny black truck pulled up as we were loading the last of my things onto our truck. She walked toward me as a guy stood beside the truck. She introduced herself and told me that he was her son, gesturing toward the man standing against the truck. I led the way inside the house and showed her the sofas, the only two things left in the living room.

She smiled and said that it was a good deal and she liked them. By this time her son entered the open front door. They talked and strategized how to get these seven-and-a-half-foot, overstuffed sofas out the door. I left them to their conversation, all the while looking at the time. My mover came in and said he was all set to go. Yes!

Except these people were struggling to even get one of the sofas out the door. It was a bit after eleven. I could still make it to my granddaughter's birthday celebration if I hurried. A stress headache kicked in. I had to be there for her. I was standing in the living room as they struggled with the sofa. Finally, desperate for some progress, I went to the moving truck and gave him the keys and the password for the storage. I had no choice. I said, "I can't leave strangers in the house." He said, "OK," and I went back inside.

Apparently the moving guy was walking behind me, because seconds later I looked up and he too was in the house. He offered to help and they twisted and turned and maneuvered the sofa in multiple positions when suddenly we heard the loud sound of glass breaking. We all covered our eyes and jumped back. Shattered glass from a light fixture was flying all around the room.

When the sound stopped I saw blood all over the floor inside and on the steps outside where the moving guy was standing. He had been hit. The three of us looked at him in shock: "Are you okay."

He lifted his bloody hand from his face, which revealed a huge gash on his forehead. By this time I was panicking, looking for anything to stop the bleeding, but everything was packed away. Finally I grabbed a sheet draped over a counter. The bleeding slowed down enough for us to look at the area. It was pretty obvious that he needed stitches.

He went to the truck to let them know he was going to the hospital to get stitched up. "Is all of this really happening? Really!"

I went to the truck to offer my support and concern. Who knows what I really said. I thought I was dreaming. He told me someone would be at the storage facility to unload my things while he's at the hospital or urgent care. He drove off and I went back inside to tell them if the sofas aren't out, just forget it. I have to get to the storage facility. It must have been something about the events that took place. They had one sofa out, and had the second one just about through the door.

"Great! Go! Leave! I can't take anymore. Please stop all this craziness. I'm leaving!" I think I said it out loud, but I'm not sure. They got the sofa out the door, and I locked up the house and was in my car before they could pull away. *I'm so over all of this.*

The storage place was 1.8 miles away. Before I could even get there I got a call from the mover. There was a lock already on my unit and they can't unload my things. I said I would stop at the office. I was almost there.

He said, "No one is in the office. I checked."

Are you freaking kidding me? My stomach immediately knotted up. Here we go again. Am I the star of this movie! Every minute a new situation.

I pulled into the parking lot at the storage facility, and there is a sign on the door that says they'd be back at 9:30. It was already noon! Is anyone actually coming back? I checked the office hours. It was Sunday, and they were supposed to be open until five PM.

The injured mover had left, and three new guys had arrived. I took the elevator to the second floor, and sure enough they hadn't taken their lock off so I could put mine on. I went back outside to speak with the movers. I asked if anyone had something to cut the lock off, and all three said no. It was 100 degrees outside. I was pacing and calling the office, hoping calls were being transferred to another public storage location. I called the other public storage, but no one was picking up.

I left messages all over Tennessee public storage for assistance. Now my daughter started calling me.

"Where are you? Is everything okay?"

I said, "Hell no! It's a hot mess at the moment!"

I briefly explained the morning's series of events, and you could hear her holding her breath in silence. She asked, "Did you eat anything?"

"No, I haven't had time. Too stressed," I told her.

I said good-bye, because I had to talk to the movers. I said, "Put the things in the hall outside my storage. I don't know what else to do."

Looking back, I wonder if I had hesitated, would I have had them take it all back to the house? Honestly, I couldn't afford it. They loaded all my things outside my indoor storage. Everything was right there in the hall, exposed. It could be taken by anyone. The bonus was that it was an extremely hot Sunday, and fewer than five people showed up that day. From the safety standpoint, it was dangerous to be alone in the building. The lights were on sensors, so there was light only where I was standing.

The movers had completed their part, and still no one had shown up at the office, yet. Before they left one of the movers walked up to me and said, "You seem like a nice lady. Be careful. There are a lot of wolves out there."

As he walked away to get into the truck with others, a skinny white guy walked up holding a brown paper bag. He didn't look up and make eye contact either with me or with the mover guy. I thought this is just great. A creepy guy, and I'm out here in the freaking heat with all my things in the hallway.

The guy walked up and hit a number on the panel to use the elevator. Well at least he had a storage unit. Someone must know who he was. We were both on camera and logged as being here, in case anything happened. But I was still waiting outside until he came out before I went back to my things. He came right back just in time to see the movers drive off. I entered my code, now that the creepy guy was walking away.

The doors opened, and I got on the elevator. I looked up, and he was rushing to get back on the elevator with me. I said to myself, "Now, if he gets on with my code instead of his, he's not here. I was trying to push the doors to close them faster. I yelled, "You're not getting on here!"

The door closed, and I was headed back to the 2nd floor—alone and in the dark. What the hell was I thinking? No other cars were even there besides mine. I had to go back down and pray to God I could beat his ass. I was nervous and weak; I hadn't eaten a bite of anything all day. My pepper spray was on a box in the hall. I was as prepared as I could be when the elevator doors opened.

Whew! He wasn't there! Then I saw my daughter pulling into the parking lot. She brought me a Starbuck's drink and a croissant. My nerves were so shot I have no idea how I was functioning. By now it's after 2:00 PM.

My daughter knew that I had zero energy. I was skeptical to eat the croissant, because it might weigh me down after running on empty for so long. She took over and started calling. By then I had reached someone at a public storage, and they were trying to find someone to help me.

While my daughter and I were both making calls separately, pacing back and forth, a car pulled in. But it wasn't help. Instead, it was someone else looking for an office employee. Interesting. He said that no one being in the office had happened before. Then another car pulled in saying that they were locked out of their storage unit, too.

Now there were three of us waiting. My daughter finally got through to someone who gave her the district manager's number. The woman I had reached earlier called me to say someone was on the way.

Somehow the heat exhaustion made me so weak I dropped my cell on the burning hot concrete and shattered my phone as it was ringing. I picked it up and could hear a voice. I said, "Yes. Hello."

It was the mover guy who went to get stitches. He said, "Are you okay? Did anybody in the office show up?"

I told him that someone was supposed to be on the way. He asked if I needed help putting my things into the unit. My eyes started to tear up, and my mouth quivered.

I said that yes, I could really use some help if he was willing.

He said, "I'll be there in a few minutes."

The next car that pulled in was a public storage employee. By then it was around three o'clock or so. She apologized and explained that the girl who was due in the office decided to quit. She never showed up for work.

As we approached my unit I started telling the woman about the weird white guy, and without my saying much more, she described him to me, and I said yes that's him. She went on to say she caught him sleeping in the hall. She took the lock off and opened my unit. I started to put things in all by myself.

My daughter had to get back to the birthday festivities. I felt bad I had missed everything. Missed my granddaughter, lunch, laughter, horseback riding, and her happy face opening her gifts. It was a pretty big disappointment.

I was stacking boxes. I wasn't mad, just relieved and glad to be moving forward again. When the moving guy showed up, I was very grateful! With his help, we were done in half an hour. After all we did have a system. We had worked together loading at the house.

It was around 4:30 when I got in my car. I just sat for a minute. Thinking about my life. I closed my eyes and took a deep breath and sighed. Then I got back out of the car to go inside the office. I went inside to thank her for coming to let me in, went back to my car and got in.

I was headed to Home Depot to replace the light fixture that had been destroyed, and to get some food to eat on the way. In the parking lot at Home Depot I made calls with my cracked phone, which is not as easy as it sounds.

I had to be patient and manipulate functions to make a call. Again, I was just grateful to have a signal. After I made a call, I grabbed some chicken for dinner. When I pulled up to the house, a sadness came over me. I had no idea what I was going to do. I was expecting another grandchild any day now in Wisconsin, which was nine or ten hours away. What I did know was that I was definitely going to meet my new grandbaby. The rest I would just have to figure out after that.

I went home, and once inside, opened my laptop, popped in a DVD, and sat down to eat. It was by then around 7:30. I was totally exhausted, and very uncomfortable. My spirit was unsettled, so much so in fact, that I decided I would leave at sunrise and head for Wisconsin.

I started to eat, finally, and to watch a movie. About twenty minutes into the movie, I heard a noise. It sounded like water dripping, but I hadn't turned on any water. What the hell? It wasn't hard to hear it, since the house was empty. I looked in the living room, but saw nothing. Then I tried the dining room, and I saw water dripping from the ceiling. What? It was in the far corner. Where could it be coming from? There wasn't any water in the area above it, and it wasn't even raining. It was a light dripping, and I said out loud, "I'm leaving. I can't even eat my food in piece."

I took a deep breath and continued eating. Now this part I had to record with my phone. Then I heard a louder dripping noise. I looked in the dining room and saw a new leak. This time it was in the middle of the ceiling. Now I was scared, but laughing, too. What the hell was going on?

All these leaks going at the same time! Again, I said, "I'm leaving," but this time I said, "I'm leaving in the morning."

Lord Jesus! I went upstairs to see if the water was somehow left on when the moving guy went up stairs to a different bathroom when he was bleeding. Even still that bathroom is on the opposite side of where the water was leaking.

I checked. No water on. I went back downstairs and sat down again to finish eating. I couldn't think a single positive, or even a complete thought at this point. My nerves were frazzled as if I drank a pot of coffee on an empty stomach.

When I went to the kitchen, I decided to get all the garbage ready and put it at the patio door. I packed my car with my suitcase and personal items and took out all the trash. Ironically I finally had a trash can dropped off on Friday and here I was moving out on Sunday.

As I write this, I realize that I have to share my stories with others. It's hard for me to believe my life sometimes. I did a final walk-through before closing my eyes for a while, especially before putting an already exhausted body on the road for ten hours tomorrow.

Before I closed my eyes, I heard a noise. Something hit the floor. Of course, I went into the dining room, since that's where all the action had been. Well, now the set is complete. A third leak has spouted, perfect trifecta…beginning, middle, and end leaks…small, medium, and this third leak is dripping so bad that paint is actually falling from the ceiling. I have video of it! I'm numb and speechless. I'm too drained to attempt to make sense out of it. Simply put: *I'm not supposed to be here.*

My cell rang and I told the caller to give me a minute to call back to escape the continuous call-dropping headache. I sat in my car and called back. It was a guy I had met back in California. He asked, "So what's going on with you?"

"You don't really want me to answer that," I said. We talked until after midnight. When we hung up, I was relaxed, and that's when I asked myself, "Why go back in the house?" No answer appearing, I drove away and headed to Wisconsin to meet my new grandchild. From there I had to make my way back to California. I had left there too soon. I had left a good life in hopes of finding a better one closer to my family, but that's not how it went down. Not by a long shot.

Of Bats and Bathtubs

By the time I got to Wisconsin, I had very little money. Actually, almost none. Even though my ex husband was 60k in arrears for back support, had no reason to believe I'd get it anytime soon. I couldn't find work in previous years when I lived in Wisconsin, I was very hopeful that I would find it easier to get work now, because I needed money so badly. My cell phone bill and my car insurance were both due. Everything was due, in fact. I started having headaches, which was rare for me. It was the stress of not having money and trying to figure out how to get some. Yesterday!

Being a massage therapist in a racist state that never utilized my service was a mental challenge. I found a worldwide site for professionals of all backgrounds to post their profiles and services. However, it wasn't free. You have to spend money to make money, which was a terrifying option for me at that moment. I took a chance, but when I did the business profile, I did not post my picture, because I am of color, and I was in a racist state, and I'm spending money to get work. I didn't want to lessen my chances even more.

During this time, I was sleeping on the couch at my daughter's house. I had my headphones on, listening to meditation affirmations and music to fall asleep. It was about one AM when she woke me up, yelling across the room, because something was in the house.

I jumped up, startled, because her voice was in a panic. When I looked up, I saw something on the ceiling going back and forth against the walls. I said, "What is that? A bird? How did a bird get in the house?"

She said, "I don't think it's a bird. It looks more like a bat!" That freaked us both out.

I had heard something in my room. I didn't pay too much attention to it right away, but the noise kept happening. I was standing there watching this thing, this bat, go from wall to wall extremely fast. I was pretty sure that the bat was just as scared of us as we were of it.

I was thinking, "Oh my gosh! Are you kidding me?" I was so overwhelmed. The funny thing was that it didn't affect me the way it might have affected most people to wake up to a bat in the house at one AM. It was almost as if *I expected it.* Damn!

Then I thought, "I'll grab a broom to try to knock it down!" What the hell I was going to do with it once I knocked it down, I had no idea. I took a swing and I hit it, but nothing happened. It just kept on flying.

The second time I swung at it, the bat fell to the floor. I saw this thing, this blackbird, still alive on the floor, and I thought, "Okay. Now what do I do?"

It just layed there, and my daughter never even came into the room, because she was afraid of it. But she did Google "bats," and learned that it's illegal to kill a bat. When she said that, I said, "Well what am I supposed to do with it, then? It's one AM. Who's going to come and get it?"

I grabbed a can of bug spray. It was the first thing I could find. It was at least good enough to keep it down and immobilized. Because I didn't know what else to do, I just covered it with a pail, put two big bottles of laundry soap on top of it to hold it in place, and went back to sleep.

My daughter left a message for the leasing office, letting them know there was a bat in the house and that they had to send someone to get it as soon as possible.

The next morning I heard a noise coming from the pail. This damn bat was still alive, and now he was angry, to boot, because he'd been covered with the pail all night. That was so crazy to me!

Well, we had to wait until the leasing office sent someone to pick it up. I was outside when the guy showed up. He got out of the truck, and he said, "Hey, are you the lady with the bat?

I started laughing, and said, "Yes." I told him that when we had called, we thought the bat was dead, but that it was still alive.

41

He said, "Are you shitting me?" There's a live bat in the house?"

I said, "Yes."

He said, "They didn't tell me that. I thought it was dead. I never handled a bat before. What the hell am I supposed to do with it?"

So we went into the house, and I showed him the bat. The bat was black, and the pail was clear, so you could see him going crazy flying around in circles inside it.

The guy said, "What the f***! You have got to be kidding me! It *is* a bat!"

I said, "If you're not sure what to do, we have to figure something out, because we don't want it loose in the house."

He said, "You don't trust me?" But he said it with a chuckle.

I said, "No. I just don't want you to let it out in the house."

He took the "For Rent" sign that he had grabbed from another property, and slid it under the pail. The bat almost got out twice. It was the scariest thing. Once he got cardboard under the pail with the bat in it, he started to walk to the door. I had already opened the door, and he walked out. He said he was a little nervous as he left. I closed the door behind him and I never saw him or the bat again, thank goodness.

I don't know what he did with it. I'm assuming he let it loose somewhere else in the city. If I had not seen it and then seen it again in the morning. I would've believed I fell asleep listening to the TV.

But that wasn't my last little adventure. Some time later I was getting ready to take a bath. Before I got in the tub I wanted to take the fan out of the window. As I started to do that, I heard someone talking. It sounded as if they were talking to me, which was weird, because I was on the upper level.

Because I had nothing on but a towel, since I was getting into the bathtub, I didn't look out the window. A few minutes later I went back so I could adjust the blinds, because they were still up a little, and when I did that, I heard someone yell, "Hey! Hey!"

This time I looked out the window thinking it was someone I knew trying to get in the house or something. I looked out and there was this guy standing in the yard. He asked me if the address was blah blah blah. I said, "No. You have the wrong house.

He went on to ask, "Are you sure?"

I said, "Yes. I know the address of the house I'm in. Who are you looking for?"

He said they were doing work for the landlord. I told him that he was at the wrong house, that there was no work order for this address. He said, "Okay."

I closed the window, put the blinds down, and turned on Pandora so I could listen to some music. Then I got back into the bathtub. I kid you not, I was in the bathtub maybe two or three minutes before I heard two sets of footsteps coming up the back stairs. They were heavy footsteps, so I knew these were the footsteps of men, and there were two sets of them. That made me jump out of the bathtub, snatch the towel that was sitting on the toilet, grab my phone, and immediately called 9-1-1.

Before I could finish telling the dispatcher my address, there was a hard knocking on the front door. I yelled, "Who is it?"

A man's voice answered, "Ma'am you are not supposed to be here."

I said, "What are you talking about? You have the wrong house."

He said, "We're here to do work for the landlord."

I said, "I told the other guy that he had the wrong house."

He went on to say that I was not supposed to be there, and that the police were coming.

I said, "You got that right, because I have the police on the phone right now."

That's when the door opened. I was still holding my cell phone with police dispatch on the line, and she could hear everything that was happening.

I said, "This man just walked in and opened the door, and I'm standing here with no clothes on. I told him he has the wrong house, but he doesn't believe me."

I also said repeatedly that I had heard two sets of footsteps. "The other person isn't showing his face, but I know he didn't leave, because I didn't hear his footsteps go back down the stairs."

The dispatcher said to put the phone on speaker so that they could hear her.

She said, "Sir, you need to leave. There is a squad car downstairs." She went on to say, "This woman says she has no clothes on. You need to leave right now."

The guy put his hands up in the air as if the police could see him, saying he wasn't trying to violate me. The other guy was still on the stairs at this time. He still hadn't left. He did say something, because he didn't know if the police were going to see him at the bottom of the stairs or not. But because I said it was two sets of footsteps, eventually he had to let it be known that he was there, too.

So they finally went back downstairs, because the police are down there, waiting to talk to them. By now I was putting my clothes on as fast as I could. There was a knock at the door before I could make it down the stairs, and it was the guy who I spoke to out the window, the same guy I told he had the wrong address. He apologized and admitted that they had the wrong address. He tried to make a joke of the other guy saying he was in an accident and that he has some loose screws. I didn't find it at all funny. Thirty minutes or so later, I saw them cleaning out the house next door.

I asked the Lord what good was supposed to come from that? Within moments I heard, "If you were not there, all of your things, and your daughter's things, and your grandchildren's things, would have been thrown out, because they were at the wrong house. That's what good came from that."

Home Again, Home Again

I arrived in Milwaukee just in time for the riots. It all started with another black man being shot by police. Technology lent a helping hand. Thanks to Facebook live, my daughter and I watched the scene unfold as we sat on the sofa in the living room, our eyes glued to the cell phone, waiting to see how far would the rioters go, and how close would it get to us.

As we watched businesses, gas stations, and cars go up in smoke; we had to keep checking in with my other daughter who was within a mile of where it finally stopped. Fearing for their lives, the firemen just let some buildings burn. Rioters looted, and then torched, beauty supply and auto supply stores. It was absolutely unreal!

A broadcaster driving thru the area was caught in gunfire when their car got too near the police. You could hear the closeness of the shots. The bus stops were even destroyed. A man was on TV saying he just got on his feet, and now he had lost everything again. The apartment he lived in above a business was burned. It was a sad scary time, and it gave me all the reason I needed to find my way back to California.

As I've said before, It is rare for me to get headaches, but headaches, anxiety, and red eyes were becoming a way of life for me. Being broke in a city that's filled with racial tension and rioting was the icing on the cake.

Here I was with $5 to my name, and a cell phone bill due with a midnight disconnect. I was pacing the floor and crying. I was so overwhelmed that I couldn't even think clearly.

Maybe it was a panic attack. For sure it was rock bottom! Of course, there was nowhere to go but up, but you don't see it that way when you're struggling through hard times. Tired if being tired was a gross understatement.

I managed to calm myself and sit on the floor. That's how I relax to meditate. Tears still flowing down my face, chest heaving, but slowing down a little bit, after a few deep sighs I closed my eyes. My mind and body were calm when I heard a voice say, "You have the power to speak it into existence."

I thought, Yeah! That's right! I do! That's how I lived and believed before this journey began."

I stood up and began to walk, and as I walked I started talking out loud throughout the house. Now tears were flowing down my face, because I was grateful to have acknowledged this moment of understanding the power God had given me. You'd better believe that I was using it to get back on track. I was walking thru the house speaking what I believed into existence: unexpected money, a clear path home, and work.

It was maybe thirty minutes later when I checked my email and I had a request for my services. Work! Thank you Lord! From that day on I got enough work to stay afloat, but I knew that I had to push forth even more in prayer, and that's exactly what I did.

I saw an ad for a massage therapist at a spa that also offered mobile service. That was great, because I had all my own equipment in my car to deliver massage services. I replied stating that I was willing to work nights and weekends, the hours no one else wanted. I received a "Thanks, but no thanks" reply. Money was getting scarce again by this time. I had to be calm, expect things to open up for me.

A few days later I saw the ad again. Really! What's the problem? I'm available! Give me the work! I emailed them again. This time they had added a phone number to the ad, so I could call them, too.

A woman answered and I explained I was calling about the job opening. Her tone of voice was disinterested. That's when I heard a voice saying, "She thinks you're younger than you are."

I literally said out loud, "Oh." My next sentence to her was, "Well, I'm here celebrating my new grandbaby, the tenth."

She said, "Oh. I like to hire older people. They're more dependable. When can you come in?"

I said I could come in the next day, and that was that. When I went in the next day, I gave the owner a session, and I started work later that day.

It was a great spa at a great location. I was a minority in an Asian spa. Some one walked in and said, "Hey! You're not Asian."

It was the best place I ever worked, and the women were awesome. You should've seen their faces when I knew enough Chinese to answer the question they asked about me. You can never tell what people know.

I was on call from 11 AM until 10 PM; I had 2 hours sessions quite often. I was in fabulous shape! I suggested the owner give me a Chinese name to match my hard work. Once I made enough money to drive back to California it was hard to say goodbye to them.

It felt great to have money in my pocket, in the coin holder in my car, buying what I needed without worry. They made me offers to stay there and work, and if it weren't for the snow that would soon be coming, it might have been a good idea. But I had to stay on track. By the way, having your pockets and purse overflowing is an affirmation to speak in your life. Just like kindness, love, and laughter.

Heading back to California I drove 800 miles the first day. I pulled over that night to rest at a truck stop, but I didn't sleep. It was freezing cold there in Nebraska. At least I think I was in Nebraska.

The next day I drove 1,200 miles, stopping only to get gas and go to the bathroom. No hot greasy food this time, either.

Finally, with only 200 miles to go, there in the darkness, I felt like I couldn't make it. During this trip, I was in contact with several people. But it was late, and I didn't want to bother them. So I kept on driving.

I drank coffee, listened to rap, let the window down, anything I could to stay awake. That got me 50 miles farther without feeling tired. Only 150 miles left. I felt stupid pulling over at this point. I even laughed out loud at the thought of it. I wasn't sleepy so I kept driving. Once I saw the "Leaving Nevada" and "Entering California" signs I was thrilled. Shortly after that I saw a sign that read, "Next 40 miles steep hills winding roads." Well that definitely kept me awake. The road was twisting and turning nonstop and at high speed. Sign after sign said the same thing, only the miles were different. I had no choice but to stay awake. No doubt about it: I was in the mountains.

Finally it was over. I was driving down the streets of California. I had made it! It was 4 AM when I took a bath before bed. When I opened my eyes the next morning, I asked myself, "Did all of that really happen, or was I just dreaming?" But I knew; it was as real as it gets.

I said Lord what am I suppose to do? What do you want me to do? A voice repeated familiar words…You can do what I need you to do from anywhere. It

doesn't matter where you are. Just do it!

Surely I'm not the only person to have received this message: Are you spending more time fulfilling your life's distractions than your purpose in life? Be real about your reason. What benefits you to lie to yourself?

TO LEARN MORE about Tonia's Journey, watch her video testimonial on YouTube by visiting..

Bit.ly/journeytofindme

Connect with Tonia!

EMAIL: createmanifest@createmanifest.com

FACEBOOK: Facebook.com/Create.Manifest

PERISCOPE: Periscope.tv/CreateManifest

INSTAGRAM: Instagram.com/CreateManifest

TWITTER: Twitter.com/CreateManifest1

www.ingramcontent.com/pod-product-compliance
Lightning Source LLC
Chambersburg PA
CBHW071439040426
42445CB00012BA/1395